RUBBISH AND WASTE

Sally Morgan

FRANKLIN WATTS
LONDON • SYDNEY

First published in 2008 by
Franklin Watts
338 Euston Road, London NW1 3BH

Franklin Watts Australia
Level 17/207 Kent Street, Sydney, NSW 2000

EARTH SOS is based on the series Earth Watch published by Franklin Watts.
It was produced for Franklin Watts by Bender Richardson White, P O Box
266, Uxbridge UB9 5NX.
Project Editor: Lionel Bender
Text Editor: Jenny Vaughan
Original text adapted and updated by: Jenny Vaughan
Designer: Ben White
Picture Researchers: Cathy Stastny and Daniela Marceddu
Media Conversion and Make-up: Mike Weintroub,MW Graphics,
and Clare Oliver
Production: Kim Richardson

For Franklin Watts:
Series Editor: Melanie Palmer
Art Director: Jonathan Hair
Cover design: Chi Leung

A CIP catalogue record for this book is available from the British Library.

ISBN 978 0 7496 7676 6

Dewey classification 363.7

Printed in China

Picture Credits Tony Stone Images: cover main image (Jeremy Walker)
and pages 4 (Jeremy Walker), 8 (Jay. S. Simon), 9 bottom (David
Woodfall), 12 (John Edwards), 13 top (Hans Peter Merten), 14/15
(Matthew McVay), 15 (Rich Fishman), 21 bottom (Jon Riley), 27 Greg
Pease. The Stock Market Photo Agency Inc.: pages 6, 24 (Lester
Lefkowitz), 29 top (Zefa/Joe Sohm). Ecoscene: cover top (Wayne Lawler)
and pages 1 (Jim Winkley), 4-5 (Nick Hawkes), 5 (Erik Schaffer), 10 (Ian
Harwood), 13 bottom (Bruce Harber), 19 top (Wayne Lawler), 26 (John
Farmer), 28 (Jim Winkley), 29 bottom (Kevin King). Panos Pictures: pages
14 (Chris Stowers), 17 bottom (David Reed), 18 (Arabella Cecil), 22 (Chris
Stowers), 25 top & 26-27 (Jim Holmes). Environmental Picture Library:
pages 7 (Irene Lengui). Environmental Images: 17 top (Martin Bond).
Still Pictures: pages 11 bottom (Matt Meadows), 19 bottom
(Mark Edwards), 20 (Peter Frischmuth), 21top (Nick Cobbing),
23 top (Dylan Garcia), 25 bottom (Mark Edwards). Science Photo Library:
9 top (Simon Fraser), 11 top (Martin Bond). Corbis Images: page 23
bottom (Neil Beer).

Artwork by Raymond Turvey

Franklin Watts is a division of Hachette Children's Books, an Hachette Livre
UK company.

Note to parents and teachers:
Every effort has been made by the publisher to ensure that websites listed are suitable for children, that they are of the highest educational value, and that they contain no inappropriate or offensive material. However, because of the nature of the Internet, it is impossible to guarantee that the contents of these sites will not be altered. We strongly advise that Internet access is supervised by a responsible adult.

CONTENTS

OUR WASTE

We throw things away all the time. We throw away plastic, metal, glass and paper. All over the world, people are making mountains of rubbish.

Homes and offices

Rubbish comes from all kinds of places. It comes from homes, shops, schools, offices and factories.

Waste water pouring into the sea.

Waste from industry

There are many different kinds of waste. Factories produce waste gases. There is waste from mines, because we do not use everything they produce. Waste harms the environment.

Using resources wisely

We call the materials we get from Earth natural **resources.** We can help save these by reusing and **recycling** them as much as we can. This is good for the environment.

This power station above burns coal as it makes electricity. It sends waste gases and steam into the air.

Rubbish has to be collected from our homes. This is the rubbish that comes from 20 houses in one week.

EVERYDAY WASTE

In rich countries, rubbish is collected from people's homes. A family throws away a dustbin of waste each week.

Sometimes, people dump rubbish in the countryside illegally. It looks bad, and can harm wild animals.

Reducing rubbish

A lot of the rubbish we throw away is paper and card from packaging. In Europe, there are laws to cut back on packaging. We can also cut down on waste. One way we can do this is to use kitchen waste to make **compost** for gardens.

Valuable rubbish

In poorer countries, people do not throw away things like plastic bags and bottles. They use them instead. Some people go to rubbish dumps and collect things to sell for recycling. They can use wood, tyres and even bottles and tins to help build their homes.

INDUSTRIAL RUBBISH

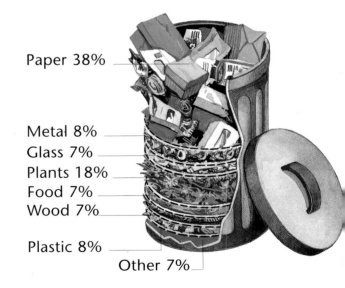

Farms 58%

Other 4%
Metals 4%
Coal 12%
Sand 3%
Wood and packaging 12%
China clay 6%
Poisonous chemicals 1%

RUBBISH FROM HOUSES

Paper 38%

Metal 8%
Glass 7%
Plants 18%
Food 7%
Wood 7%

Plastic 8%
Other 7%

These people in the Philippines are searching through rubbish. They can reuse some things to make huts to live in.

7

HOLES FOR WASTE

Rubbish is often dumped in big holes in the ground that were once quarries or gravel pits. These are called landfill sites.

A tanker pours liquid into a landfill site.

Filling holes

Rubbish takes up a lot of space. It is often squashed up, so as much as possible can fit into a **landfill site.** When the hole is full, soil is put on top. Then the land can be used.

At this landfill site in Spain, plastic sheets stop poison getting into the soil.

This bulldozer is piling up rubbish at a landfill site. Nearly all the rubbish in the world is put in landfill sites.

Landfill problems

There are problems with landfill sites. They are smelly and they look horrible. Pests such as mice, rats and birds come to the sites looking for food they can eat. Poisonous chemicals get into the soil. Sometimes, people line the landfill sites with plastic to stop this from happening.

Using gas

The rubbish in landfill sites rots and makes a gas called **methane.** This is a **biogas.** It might explode if it stays underground. So there are pipes to bring it to the top. It can be burned there, or sent to factories and used as fuel.

9

WASTE TO ENERGY

Space for landfill sites is running out. We must find other ways to get rid of rubbish. One way is to burn it.

Burning rubbish

Rubbish that is going to be burnt has to be sorted first. Some of the rubbish, such as metal and glass, can be recycled. This is taken away. The rest is put into an **incinerator**, which is a kind of oven. The waste in it is burnt.

This machine is called a rotary screen. It separates different kinds of rubbish from each other.

Eco Thought
Rubbish can make as much electricity as other fuels.

Hotting up

Burning rubbish can create a problem. It may give off harmful gases, which can get into the air. But it can also be useful. The heat from burning rubbish can be used to make electricity. The waste left behind in the incinerators can be used in road-building. Sometimes, rubbish is made into little blocks of fuel which can be burned in boilers. This is called Refuse Derived Fuel (RDF).

This fuel is made from the rubbish from people's homes. It is called RDF and it can be burnt for heating.

Producing biogas

The rotting waste in landfill sites produces methane gas. So does animal and food waste, and the waste from our own bodies. This gas can be used in homes as fuel for heating.

On the Ground

Animal waste is a good **fertilizer** for crops. In many countries, it is burned as fuel. It can even be burnt in power stations, to make electricity.

This is rubbish that is going to be used in a power station in the United States.

ELECTRICITY

We use electricity for televisions, computers, lights, and many other things. But when we make electricity, we also make waste.

Generating electricity

Making electricity is called generating it. Many power stations generate electricity by burning gas, coal or oil. These are called **fossil fuels.** Burning them gives off waste gases that make our climate warmer. We call these **greenhouse gases.**

*This power station burns fossil fuels. The heat boils water, to make steam. This spins wheels called **turbines,** which help make electricity.*

Cleaner power

Burning fossil fuels also makes a gas called **sulphur dioxide.** This makes **acid rain.** This can kill trees and harm buildings. Chimneys with special filters can stop some harmful gases getting into the air. It is better to make electricity without using fossil fuels.

This coal mine provides the power station with coal. It also leaves waste rocks which contain poisonous chemicals.

Eco Thought

Chimneys in power stations have limestone filters to stop harmful gases getting into the air. The filters make limestone waste. This is good fertilizer.

The chimney of this power station has a filter in it. It stops harmful sulphur dioxide getting into the air.

NUCLEAR FUEL

In a nuclear power station, the energy used to make electricity comes from uranium. This is a kind of metal.

Radioactive materials

Inside the power station, the **atoms** of the **uranium** are split. This makes a lot of energy. It also produces dangerous **particles,** which are **radioactive.** These can make all the waste from the power station radioactive.

Eco Thought
Old parts from nuclear power stations are very radioactive. They have to be stored safely for hundreds of years.

Radioactive substances can harm all living things, including people. So nuclear power stations must take care not to let radioactive waste get into the environment.

This is nuclear waste in Taiwan. It is stored in concrete.

In the future

Many people are afraid of nuclear power, even though new power stations are safer than older ones. Scientists are trying to find even safer ways of making nuclear power.

These drums have radioactive waste in them. They are being checked for leaks.

This waste is slightly radioactive. It has been put in drums, and will be buried in a deep pit.

Eco Thought
The worst disaster at a nuclear power station was in 1986 at Chernobyl, in Ukraine. Radioactive clouds spread across Europe.

WATER

Many factories use a lot of water, and so do farms. When factories and farms have used the water, they often empty it into rivers or the sea.

Waste from mines

Waste can get into rivers from factories, mines and power stations. So can human waste from people's toilets, and fertilizers from farms.

Warm water from power stations

Waste from factories

Fertilizers from farms

Heat pollution

Power stations use steam to turn turbines. They cool this afterwards with water. Many factories also use water for cooling. They put warm water back into rivers and the sea. Warm water does not contain much of the gas **oxygen,** which water animals need to live.

Sewage from homes

Harmful wastes

Wastes from factories and farms may contain poisons. Some contain sewage. When tiny living things called **bacteria** eat this, they use up the oxygen in the water.

Killer weed

Fertilizers and sewage in water help tiny plants called **algae** spread. They absorb light, so other plants cannot grow.

Dirty foam shows there is pollution in the sea above.

Pollution

In many countries, there are laws to stop factories from putting waste into seas and rivers. Scientists test the water to see if it is clean. Factories are fined if they pollute water. But it is hard to stop people dumping waste out at sea.

This nuclear waste is going to be dumped in the sea.

TOXIC WASTE

Some factories produce waste chemicals that are poisonous to living things. We call these chemicals toxic waste.

Buried in the ground

In the past, people used to bury **toxic** waste in the ground. Houses were built on the land. But toxic waste got into the soil and the water, and it was not safe for people to live on this land.

Eco Thought

Toxic chemicals can build up in the bodies of sea animals, such as Beluga whales. **Inuit** people hunt and eat them, and the toxic chemicals build up in their bodies, too.

This tin mine in Bolivia, South America, has closed, but its toxic waste still gets into the river.

These containers have toxic chemicals in them. These can get into the water and poison it.

PCBs

The Hudson River is in the United States. It has had toxic chemicals called **PCBs** in it for over 100 years. These are not used now, but they still get into the river from land where factories once stood. The only way to get rid of the PCBs is to dig up the mud from the riverbed.

Making soil safe

Soil with toxic waste in it must be taken away. Plants are grown on it. These take up the waste, and then they are burnt. This helps make the soil safe to use.

These scientists are testing river water for toxic chemicals. They also check that there is enough oxygen in the water.

RECYCLING WASTE

There are many ways to recycle waste. We can reuse things instead of throwing them away. Or we can use rubbish to make new things.

Recycling for building

Making new buildings uses up many natural materials we get from the Earth. These include clay for bricks, wood from trees, and rocks, metals and glass. If we recycle materials from old buildings, we do not use up the Earth's resources in this way.

These fences are made from plastic that has been recycled.

Try this

Put garden waste into a compost heap and use it on the garden, or take it to a recycling centre. It can be made into compost there.

This garden waste is being shredded. Afterwards, it will rot and turn into compost.

Problems with plastic

We are using more and more plastic. It is not easy to recycle plastic, because there are many different kinds. Each kind has to be recycled separately, and many objects are made of more than one kind of plastic. For example, a plastic bottle may contain three different kinds of plastic. It would be better if there were fewer kinds of plastic in each object.

These people are sorting plastic and glass at a recycling centre.

21

GLASS

We can use glass in many different ways. It is easy to recycle glass bottles and jars.

Recycling glass

To make glass, some sand and limestone rock are heated in a **furnace**. Liquid glass forms, and is then made into different objects. When glass is recycled, it is broken into small pieces called **cullet.** This is put in a furnace with the sand and the limestone.

The recycling plant above is in Ireland. The bottles will be sorted, and then used again.

At a recycling plant, glass of the same colour is collected. Then it is made into cullet.

Reusing bottles

It saves money and materials if we reuse glass bottles. In many places, bottles from soft drinks are collected and sent back to the factory for recycling. There, they are washed and re-filled. Bottles can be reused many times in this way.

These bottles in Mexico are made from recycled glass.

Saving materials

If we recycle glass, we use less sand and limestone. Also, cullet does not need as much heat as sand and limestone to melt. This means it uses less energy.

On the Ground

In many countries, people sort out their rubbish. This is collected every week. Some of it is taken away to be recycled. This saves both materials and energy.

METALS

Many metals can be found in the ground, mixed with other materials. This mix is called ore. It has to be separated into metal and waste rock.

This metal is rusting away. It could be recycled instead.

Melt down

Waste rock is put in heaps called **spoil heaps.** If we recycle metals, we do not take as much natural materials from under the ground. There is less waste.

Eco Thought

Making an aluminium can from **bauxite** uses 20 times more energy than recycling one.

Multi-use metal

We use aluminium for making foil, drinks cans and even furniture. It comes from a kind of ore called bauxite. Bauxite is dug up from the ground. It is heated to get the metal out of the rock.

A man chops up cans for recycling.

Try this

Test used drinks cans with a magnet. A magnet will stick to cans made from steel, but not to cans made from aluminium.

This forest in Australia is cleared away so people can dig up bauxite.

Saving forests

Each person in the United States uses about 130 drinks cans every year. These are often made of aluminium. Sometimes, forests are cut down so people can make quarries where they can dig up bauxite. If we recycle aluminium, we save forests. Melting down old cans uses less energy than making new aluminium. So recycling saves energy, too.

PAPER

Paper is made from wood. Most of this comes from conifers (fir and pine trees). But we can also make new paper by recycling old paper.

Making paper

The timber (wood) from trees goes to a pulp mill. It is chopped up into a kind of sawdust called wood pulp. This goes to a paper mill. It is mixed with water and chemicals, and then spread out. The water drains away, to leave sheets of paper. Recycled paper is made from waste paper pulp instead of wood pulp.

After these trees are cut down, new ones will be planted.

Eco Thought

Each person in the United States uses more than 300 kg of paper every year. In India, they use about 3 kg.

This truck is collecting waste paper to be recycled.

Saving energy

Recycling paper helps save trees. We can also replant the trees we chop down. We say they are a renewable resource. But these new trees are not good for wildlife. Older forests are better. Recycling paper means we can keep more older forests. Also, we do not need to plant new trees where there was once grassland, or peat bogs. So recycling means we can save wildlife. It also saves the energy that is used when trees are chopped down and taken to pulp mills.

Try this

Paper is made up of tiny fibres. Tear some paper. Look at the torn edge of the paper with a magnifying glass. Can you see the fibres?

Paper is made in giant rolls in a paper mill.

WHAT CAN WE DO?

We can all help make less waste. There are three words to help us remember how: reduce, reuse and recycle.

These children are recycling glass.

Reduce, reuse, recycle

We can all help reduce waste by only buying what we need. Making things uses up energy, so we save energy if we buy less. A lot of waste is packaging. We can buy things with less packaging, and this means we make less waste. We can also reuse things, instead of throwing them away. For example, we can reuse bottles and jars. If we cannot reuse things, we can recycle them.

Local recycling

We can collect waste and take it to a local recycling centre. Wear gloves to protect your hands from dirt, broken glass and other dangerous things.

Old clothes for new

We can take old clothes to charity shops or recycle them. Wool from old jumpers can be made into new thread. Cotton can be made into paper.

Here, people have collected dangerous waste from their homes for recycling.

Around the world

All around the world, governments are trying to cut back on waste. They are trying to recycle more. They are also trying to find better ways of getting rid of dangerous waste.

We can use kitchen waste to make compost.

FACT FILE

Scrap heap

More than two million cars are scrapped each year in the UK. The metal and some plastic is recycled.

Tyre tale

People in the United States throw away more than 250 million car tyres every year. In Europe, we throw away about 200 million. In Britain, in 2001, we threw away 50 million. We reused or recycled about half of them. The rest went into dumps or landfill sites.

In the can

In 1996, more than 32 billion steel cans were made in the United States. About half were recycled. In the UK, we only recycle about 20 per cent of our cans.

Steel appeal

Every year, about 300 million tonnes of steel is recycled. No other metal is recycled as much. Doing this saves digging up millions of tonnes of iron ore, which is used to make steel. It also saves the energy used to get the metal from the ore. About a quarter of every new steel can is recycled steel.

News on trees

People in the United Kingdom use a lot of paper every year. On average, we each use up the amount of paper we could get from two trees. Most of the paper we use is newspaper.

Websites

www.epa.gov/recyclecity

www.epa.gov/kids/garbage.htm

GLOSSARY

Acid rain Rain that is made acid by some gases given off by burning fossil fuels.

Algae Tiny water plants.

Atom The smallest part of any substance.

Bacteria Very tiny living things. Some bacteria cause disease.

Bauxite The rock that contains aluminium.

Biogas A gas made by plant and animal waste.

Compost Rotted plants which can be used as fertilizer.

Conifers Trees such as fir trees and pine trees which keep their leaves all year round.

Cullet Broken glass.

Fertilizer Substances we add to the soil to help plants grow.

Fossil fuels Fuels such as coal, oil and gas.

Furnace A kind of very hot oven, used to melt metal or glass.

Greenhouse gases Gases that trap heat in the air and keep the Earth warm.

Incinerator An oven for burning rubbish.

Inuit A group of people who live in the Arctic.

Landfill site A big hole in the ground where rubbish is put.

Methane A kind of biogas. It can be burnt as fuel.

Oxygen A gas that most living things need to survive.

Particle Very tiny part of a substance. A particle is bigger than an atom.

PCBs (Polychlorinated biphenyls) Chemicals once used in industry. They are poisonous.

Pollution Waste in the environment.

Radioactive Giving off dangerous rays called radiation.

Recycling Making new things from old or used things.

Renewable Can be replaced.

Resources Materials that we use, such as wood, metals or coal.

Sewage Human waste.

Spoil heap Piles of waste soil and rock from quarries.

Sulphur Dioxide A poisonous gas given off by burning fossil fuels.

Toxic Poisonous.

Turbines Big wheels used in power stations. As they turn, they help make electricity.

Uranium A kind of radioactive metal.

INDEX